THE FASHIONABLE LADY IN THE
19th CENTURY

VICTORIA AND ALBERT MUSEUM

THE
FASHIONABLE LADY
IN THE
19th CENTURY

by Charles H. Gibbs-Smith

LONDON
HER MAJESTY'S STATIONERY OFFICE
1960

Printed in England for Her Majesty's Stationery Office
by Butler & Tanner Ltd., Frome and London

FOREWORD

This Museum possesses one of the finest collections of original dresses, costume designs and fashion-plates, which is available to students in the Museum galleries, in the Departments of Textiles, of Engraving, Illustration and Design, the Library, and in the Bethnal Green Museum (a branch of the Victoria and Albert Museum). A small selection of nineteenth century fashion plates was published in 1947, in the form of a volume by Mr. James Laver entitled *Nineteenth Century Costume*. When this work went out of print it was thought appropriate, especially in view of the re-arrangement of the Museum's costume collections, to issue a more elaborate pictorial survey of the period, but still confining the subject to the fashionable lady in the nineteenth century. The present work has been undertaken by Mr. Charles H. Gibbs-Smith, Keeper of the Department of Public Relations and Education, with the assistance of Miss Audrey Blanshard, formerly of the same Department. Mr. Gibbs-Smith wishes to express his gratitude for their help and advice to Mr. James Laver, Mr. J. L. Nevinson, Mrs. Madeleine Ginsburg of the Department of Textiles, Mrs. Beryl Edginton, and – especially – Dr. Phillis Cunnington and to her husband the late Dr. C. Willett Cunnington.

JOHN POPE–HENNESSY
Director

INTRODUCTION

When we think of fashionable nineteenth century costume, the images in our minds are based on a mixture of memories taken from the surviving dresses, theatrical costume, family photographs, the photographs in the many 'period' books now available, contemporary paintings and prints, modern pastiches, and – perhaps the most vivid of all – the contemporary fashion plates. Although the material available on the nineteenth century is rich and varied, there has never yet been published a systematically arranged series of all types of women's costume illustrations stretching throughout the century. To make this even reasonably complete, a very large work would be necessary, a work which would include illustrations from every contemporary source, and cover all the social classes of the population. Such an undertaking would, however, be outside the scope of the Museum's publications.

So the present work has been limited to the woman of fashion, and to the illustration of her clothes chiefly through the medium of the fashion plate. These limitations inevitably impose a certain idealised artificiality on the subject, but at the same time there is an advantage in the uniformity of treatment. The fashion plate, whatever its disadvantages, at least shows what the fashion designers were putting forth as the ideal to be aimed at by fashionable women, even though the majority of them were unable to afford such dresses, and – even if they could – would in most cases fall far short of the fashion plates in beauty and elegance. In practice, the fashion plates were followed by a few women, partly imitated by many, and – often with a year or two's time-lag – echoed by a large number of women, the echoes growing fainter as the time-lag increased.

The fashion plates therefore provide a series of stylised ideal dresses, often of much elegance in themselves, which will always provide an attractive reflection of what the women of the time felt to be the height of fashion. They will always, one feels, appeal to the student, designer and the general public alike.

In the present work I have taken the first year of every half-decade throughout the century – ending with 1900 for convenience – and placed there a selection of both day and evening dresses, and illustrations of corsets where it has been possible to find them; in addition, at the end of each of these half-decade sections, one or two fashionable scenes have been included, as drawn or painted by contemporary artists: the latter, which include a few caricatures, were not always made at the exact date, but reflect the fashionable dress of the time to within a year or two. In this way, it is hoped that the reader will be able to appreciate the full stream of nineteenth century fashion, both as worn during the day and in the evening, evenly spaced over the years, to show the development of line and style.

Only the fashions of the 'beau monde' are shown in the illustrations, for to include the 'aesthetic' and other deviations of dress, and the many subsidiary types of clothes – bathing, riding, sporting, cycling, etc. – would have been impracticable in a work of this kind.

In order to make the book of more interest to the general reader, I have included a short description of the fashion characteristics of each half-decade. Immediately preceding the illustrations is a series of line drawings to show the predominant 'line' of each half-decade; and give a bird's eye view of the development of the styles throughout the whole century.

DESCRIPTIVE COMMENTARY

1800–1810

The predominant character of the line in the early years of the century in France and England is classical, with a high waist and the skirt hanging loosely down to the ground. In France, the waist was immediately below the bust; in England, due to lack of communication with Paris, the waist-line often dropped almost to true waist level. By 1810 the skirts, although still loose and long, were just clear of the ground. The short jacket known as the 'spencer' was popular during this decade.

1815

Waists are still medium high or very high, but skirts are often gored, and tend to flare slightly towards the hem, the effect being accentuated by flouncing: the hem-line is well above the ground, revealing the feet. More emphasis is being placed on the shoulders, aided by the puffed sleeves.

1820

Waists are high, or medium high, with an occasional drop to an almost normal waist. The slightly flaring skirts are becoming somewhat fuller; the fullness at the back is noticeable, and is helped by the tying of a small bustle – a roll or pad – underneath the skirt at the back of the waist. The hem is still well off the ground. Shoulders are more accentuated than ever. The pelisse-robe is much worn at this time.

1825

All waist-lines are medium low; skirts are longer and – owing to the more normal and pronounced waist – tend to flow out into a wide bell-shape: the waist is often emphasised by a broad sash or belt. A particular feature of day dresses is the full sleeve, particularly the 'gigot', which is very full above, and tapering below, the elbow.

1830

In the intervening five years, women's costume has rapidly evolved into an exuberant and romantic affair, characterised by enormous hats and sleeves, balanced by shorter and more pronounced bell-skirts below the tightly-laced normal waist-lines. Stockings embroidered up the calf are often worn.

1835

The same enormous sleeves, tight waists, and large bell-shaped skirts – the latter now longer – are fashionable; but the whole character of the day dresses has been changed by the complete disappearance of the great hats, and the substitution of oval bonnets. Evening dresses generally substitute large puffed sleeves for the full-length sleeves.

1840

Another of fashion's abrupt and unheralded changes occurred in 1836, when the great sleeves of the early thirties suddenly collapsed, and thus – a year before Queen Victoria's accession – women's dress began to assume its typical 'early Victorian' look: an appearance of prim sentimentality takes the place of the romantic exuberance, of which perhaps the popular hair-style of ringlets is typical. By this year, 1840, the skirts still 'sprout out' and swell dome-shaped to the ground; a tight-fitting bodice rises from a tight-fitting waist: the emphasis is on the shoulders, with a slight droop of the shoulder-line; and sleeves are narrower. The ubiquitous bonnet is becoming smaller and rounder. The shawl is becoming popular.

1845

The primly sentimental phase is now at its height: fashion has slowed up, and will remain more or less static until the late 1850's. Skirts remain full, and bodices tight-fitting. The general feeling of sentimentality in the styles is conveyed by an increased drooping of the shoulder-line; and, in evening dresses, by the growing popularity of the 'bertha': this was a broad horizontal draping of the bust, often flounced with a fall of lace or other material, some three or four inches deep. Evening skirts are often boldly flounced. The shawl is now a feature of day dresses, as are 'pardessus' and other mantles in winter.

1850

Here is the high point of what many people – wrongly, I think – consider typical Victorian dress: it is really only the climax of *early* Victorian dress. The word one so often hears applied to the skirts – 'crinoline' – is actually a misnomer, as crinoline was originally only the name of a fabric of horse-hair (from the French *crin* – horse-hair), or later other stiffened fabrics such as silk, cotton or linen, used as a foundation beneath a hem or a sleeve. The word had long been in use – it appears at least as early as 1829 – for a lining-strip for day skirts. Now, in 1850, and for the next five years, the word 'crinoline' comes to imply the whole typical dome-shaped skirt, whose shape was preserved by the incorporation of some crinoline, or other stiffening fabric, in the outermost of the multiple petticoats; petticoats could number up to six until 1856. Modern usage of the word 'crinoline' is even looser, and implies almost any wide skirt kept out by any means, including hoops. The bodice is still tight-fitting, the sleeves are still narrow, and the shoulders still droop. The small bonnet remains universal. For daytime wear, the shawl and the various kinds of mantle and cloak are also universal. For evening dress, the 'bertha' and the heavily flounced skirt are particularly favoured.

1855

The skirt is now swelled out to the maximum capacity which the materials, the flounces, the under-stiffening, and the multiple petticoats, can produce. The dome-like look of the skirts has given way to a huge fan-like silhouette, with a tendency to expand behind more than elsewhere. Mantles and cloaks serve to enhance the overall size. Bodices, 'berthas', and the shoulder-line, remain mostly constant; but sleeves are becoming fuller. Bonnets are at last becoming smaller, and slipping backwards to frame the head rather than cover it. The general air of sentimentality of the previous decade is disappearing.

1860

Another vital and sudden innovation had taken place in the invention of the so-called 'artificial crinoline' in 1856. When skirts had apparently reached their apogee in size, there arrived the means to expand them even more. The 'artificial crinoline' consisted of concentric whale-bone, wire, or watch-spring hoops suspended on strips of material, with or without covering fabric. Not only has the contour and outline of the skirt changed, but its character and movement is transformed. It tends now to swing attractively from the waist, as the multiple petticoats have disappeared. The 'artificial crinoline' has also done away with the small bustle formerly used to throw the skirt out at the back. By 1858–60 the fashionable lady has become so gigantic that further expansion is now literally impossible if she is to move about at all. There is already a tendency for the front of the skirt to flatten, and the back to arch farther out: the rest of the costume, dominated by the skirt, remains fairly constant, with sleeves becoming still fuller. The off-the-face bonnet is still much in vogue.

1865

The mountainous skirt of 1860, at last unable to expand any further for purely 'navigational' reasons – yet still determined to survive – has retreated rearwards. The front is becoming still flatter, and the back still more voluminous, even to the point of resembling a train: the sides, too, are still voluminous. The bodice is tending to shorten, with a higher waist.

1870

The so-called 'crinoline style' began going out of fashion about 1865, and it disappeared so fast that, by this year 1870, the first full bustle phase has arrived. The great skirt of the 1860's has become more and more flattened in the front, and more bunched-up behind, with elaborate 'bouffant' trimmings and flounces. The sides of the skirt are now narrowing, and tend to follow more closely the curves of the hips. Fashionable dress has taken on a 'front-and-back' accentuation. Much of the structure of this fashion depends on the revival of the bustle, which was originally a small pad or roll, and is now a shaped framework held on by a tape round the waist, over which the bunched skirt is draped. As if to complement the bustle, hats tend to be worn tilted forward on the front of the head.

1875

The changes in style are again clearly defined, and the chief features is now the suppression of the bustle by means of the tightly fitting 'cuirasse bodice', which is often similar to the current corsets. The 'cuirasse bodice' gives the waist tight but gracefully designed curves, and at this time extends only a short way over the hips, often dipping both at front and back: the latter serves to reduce the size of the tie-back skirt. There is also a general tightening of the skirt around the hips. Sleeves are sometimes fuller. Hats are small and still often tilted forward over the brow.

1880

The bustle, which was subdued by 1875, has completely disappeared, but will – strangely enough – reappear later: it has been only temporarily suppressed. The corset-like 'cuirasse bodice', which had imposed itself on fashion by 1875, now encases the whole torso, like an armoured sheath, giving the body a smooth and elegant shape, with a well-defined waist and pronounced curves, and only allowing the skirt to escape below the hips. In evening dresses the length of the 'cuirasse bodice' tends to be somewhat shortened to balance the décolletage, but not always. When coats are worn over the day dresses, they tend either to imitate the 'cuirasse bodice', or to encase the whole body from neck to feet. Tailor-made costumes in cloth first appear between 1875 and 1880. Also appearing during the 1870's (not illustrated here) is the loose tea-gown, worn without a corset.

1885

The bustle, as if driven out of fashion reluctantly by the 'cuirasse bodice' – but still determined on survival – has not only returned now after only a few years' eclipse, but returned in a fantastically exaggerated form: yet despite its oddity, it exerts a certain fascination. Even the stance of the figure adapts itself to show off this new creation, for the style encourages the bust to be thrown forward, and the head held back. The enormous bustle tends to arch up and away from the back, before plunging down to the ground, giving the impression that the woman is saddled with a shrouded bird cage which sticks monstrously out behind her. The bodice is still closely moulded to the waist and bust. The day dresses of the mid-1880's are mainly heavy and enveloping, whereas the evening dresses tend to be sleeveless and exhibit extreme décolletage.

1890

The exaggerated bustle of the mid-1880's has disappeared almost as rapidly as it had arrived; and by this year 1890, a complete transformation has taken place. Although still tending to fullness at the back, the skirt – despite draping – has narrowed overall, with no true bustle: it is surmounted by a new conception of the bodice. The hip-line is made to close in sharply over the waist, and then the bodice rises long and slender to the bust and shoulders: here the leg-of-mutton sleeves are developing – which 'sprout' high above the shoulders – giving the curious impression that the arms have been fixed to pivots, as on a lead soldier. The new bodice-forms are well shown in the lines of the current corsets. In the evening dresses, with their extreme décolletage, the leg-of-mutton sleeves disappear; but they are symbolised, as it were, by 'sproutings' of materials, or other ornamental additions, attached to the shoulder straps; or, if worn, to the very short sleeves. There is, curiously enough, considerably more trace of the bustle-fullness surviving in the evening skirts than in the day skirts.

1895

Yet another total transformation of style has been effected in half a decade; by this year 1895, the leg-of-mutton sleeves have already swelled into enormous puffed sleeves reminiscent of 1830, although the leg-of-mutton origin is still occasionally apparent. The effect of the sleeves is enhanced, and even exaggerated, by the almost universal accentuation of the narrow waist by sashes or belts: this practice is varied in some evening dresses by the wearing of a tight, stiff bodice. In contrast, skirts have become simple and severe: they are mostly gored, and 'flare out' equally all round as if to balance the immensity of the shoulder-line. Hats, too, have grown in size and complexity, to match the shoulders. In evening dresses, the daytime style is preserved almost intact by retaining the huge sleeves: these are individually accentuated by the décolletage, which serves to separate and isolate them. The evening skirts, like those of the daytime, are comparatively severe.

1900

The great puffed sleeves of the mid-decade have vanished as rapidly as they appeared. Sleeves have, in fact, become tight about the whole arm, except at the shoulders, where a slight fullness – or epaulet effect – is sometimes seen. This tightness of the sleeves, and the still extreme tightness of the waist, serves to accentuate the two equally dominating features of this style, the bust and hips. The bust, thrown forward by the construction of the corset, has become the so-called 'monobosom', denying anatomy and monopolising virtually the whole of the front of the bodice; this effect is exaggerated by the forward-leaning stance, the tight lacing, and the tightness of the skirt over the hips. Skirts, day and evening, all exhibit this tightness at the hips: the tightness extends down almost to the knees, and then flares to the ground, sometimes with a slight train, the flare often accentuated by flounces or other decoration. Evening dresses follow the same lines as the day dresses.

NOTE ON COLOUR

The important subject of the colours favoured in nineteenth century fashions is dealt with in detail in Dr. C. Willett Cunnington's *English Women's Clothing in the Nineteenth Century* (see bibliography), especially on pages 14–18.

The number in parentheses at the end of each caption is the official photograph number which should always be quoted when ordering prints. Where such numbers are not given, photographs cannot be supplied.

1800 1805 1810 1815 1820

1845 1850 1855

1875 1880 1885

1825   1830   1835   1840

1860   1865   1870

1890   1895   1900

1800

1. 1800. Morning dresses. (R.802)

2. 1800. Morning costumes. (R.801)

3. 1800. Morning costumes. (R.804)

4. 1800. Evening dresses. (R.803)

5. 1801. Evening dress. (R.1276)   **6.** 1801. Evening dress. (R.1277)

7–9. 1802. Boodle's Club fête to George III (details).
10. 1800. *Parisian ladies in their Winter dress* (caricature, detail). (R.1135)

II. 1802. *Promenade de Longchamps* (detail). (R.1057)

1805

12. 1805. Morning and evening dress. (R.813)

13. 1805. Walking dresses and a full evening dress. (R.812)

14. 1805. Afternoon dresses. (R.1139)

15. 1805. Walking costume. (R.1138)

16. 1805. Full evening dress. (R.1140)

17. 1805. Full evening dress and walking dress. (R.1143)

18. 1805. Walking costume. (R.1141)

19. 1805. Full evening dress (Parisian). (R.1278)

20. 1805. Scene at Vauxhall Gardens (detail). (R.699)

1810

21. 1810. Morning dress. (R.805)

22. 1810. Carriage or promenade costume. (R.807)   **23.** 1810. Promenade costumes. (R.811)

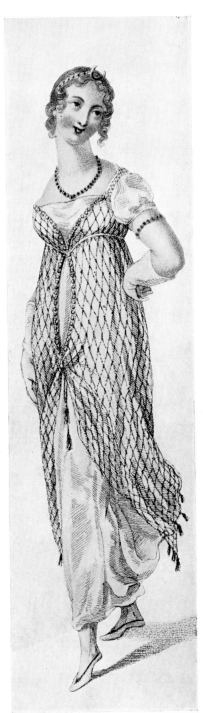

24. 1810. Full evening dress. (R.810)

25. 1810. Ball dress. (R.808)

26. 1810. Evening dress. (R.806)

27. 1810. Ball dress. (R.809)

28, 29. 1810. Corset (French).   **30.** 1810. Corset (English) (detail). (R.947)

31. c.1809. Corsets (French).

32. 1810. *The Graces in a high wind.* (R.1190)

33. 1812. The Rivals. (R.1134)

1815

34. 1815. Morning dress. (R.794)

35. 1815. Walking costume. (R.798)   **36.** 1815. Walking costume. (R.797)

39

37. 1815. Ball dress. (R.793)

38. 1815. Walking costume. (R.792)

40

39. 1815. Evening dress. (R.795)   **40.** 1815. Full evening dress. (R.800)

41

41. 1815. Walking costume. (R.796)

42. 1813. *The Breakfast* (detail). (R.1274)   **43.** 1813. *The Library* (detail). (R.1275)

44. 1816. *La famille Anglaise à Paris.* (R.1058)
45. 1814. *Le Bon Genre* (caricatures).

1820

46. 1820. Walking costume. (R.775)

47. 1820. Day dress. (R.764)   **48.** 1820. Walking dress. (R.774)

49. 1820. Walking costume. (R.768)

50. 1820. Walking costume. (R.766)

51. 1820. Ball dress. (R.773) **52.** 1820. Evening dress. (R.767)

53. 1820. Full evening dresses. (R.765; R.769)

54. 1821. *Tom and Jerry . . . at the Royal Academy* (detail). (R.826)

55. 1821. *Tom and Jerry in the Saloon at Covent Garden* (detail). (R.825)

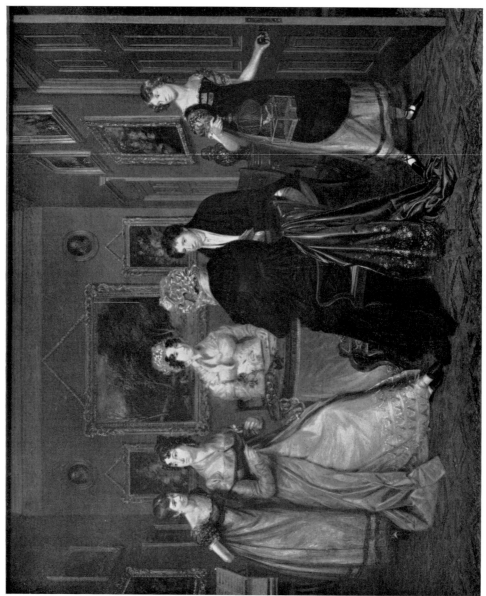

56. 1822. *The Cooke family.*

1825

57. 1825. Morning dress. (R.780)

58. 1825. Promenade costume. (R.944)　　　　**59.** 1826. Promenade costume (R.776)

60. 1825. Morning dress. (R.778)   **61.** 1825. Evening dress. (R.781)

62. 1825. Evening dress. (R.945)   **63.** 1825. Ball dress. (R.777)

64. 1825. Full evening dress. (R.779)

65, 66. 1826. Scene at the Royal Wells, Cheltenham (details). (R.824)

67. 1826. The Cyprians Ball at the Argyll Rooms. (R.823)

1830

68. 1830. Carriage, dinner, and promenade costumes. (R.827)

69. 1830. Dinner dress; evening dress; ball dress. (R.828)

70. 1830. Evening dress and full evening dress. (R.829)

71. 1830. Evening dress and morning dress. (R.831)

72. 1830. Evening dress and opera dress. (R.832)

73. 1830. Corset.

74. 1830. Corset.

75. *c.*1830. *At the Shoemaker's.*

76. 1827. *Nothing extenuate, nor ought set down in malice* (caricature). (R.1189)

77. 1828. *A lively idea* (caricature). (R.1187)

78. 1829. *The great boa tippet* (caricature). (R.1185)

79. c. 1830. *Can't you look the other way now* (caricature). (R.1186)

1835

80. 1835. Day dresses. (R.816)

81. 1835. Promenade costumes. (R.815)

82. 1835. Carriage costumes. (R.817)

83. 1835. Ball dresses. (R.818)

84. 1835. Ball dress. (R.814)

85. 1837. Corset.

86. 1835. Promenade costumes. (R.1059)

87. 1833. The opening of the New Hungerford Market (detail).

88. 1833. *The Grosvenor family.*

1840

89. 1840. Day dresses. (R.906)

90. 1840. Promenade dresses. (R.820)

91. 1840. Carriage costumes. (R.908)

92. 1840. Evening dress (and "burnouse"). (R.946)

93. 1840. Ball dresses. (R.819)

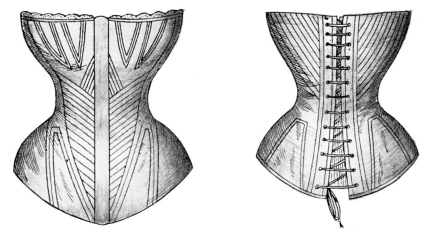

94, 95. 1840. Corset (front and back).

96. 1842. *Hyde Park, near Grosvenor Gate* (detail). (R.749)

97. 1840. Musical evening party (detail).

1845

98. 1845. Outdoor costume and indoor dress. (R.880)

99. 1845. Promenade costume and day dress. (R.877)

100. 1845. Promenade costumes. (R.879)

101. 1845. Promenade costumes. (R.878)

102. 1845. Evening dresses. (R.876)

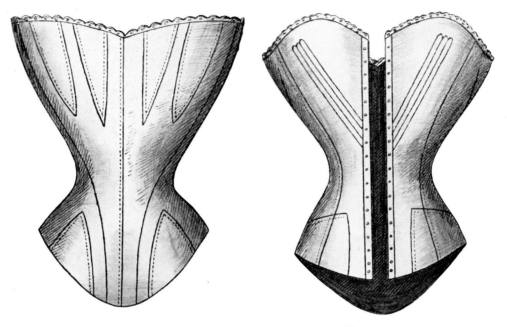

103, 104. 1845. Corset (front and back).

105. 1845. *Thé Dansante.* (R.897)

106, 107. 1845. Horticultural fête in the grounds of Downing College, Cambridge (detail).
(R.899)

108. 1850. Day dresses. (R.882)

109. 1850. Day costumes. (R.870)

110. 1850. Promenade costumes. (R.884)

111. 1850. Full evening dresses. (R.869)

112. 1850. Full evening dresses. (R.1279)

113. (left) 1850. Corset.

114. (below) 1850. Corset.

115. 1851. Taking refreshments at the Great Exhibition of 1851 (detail). (J.294)

116. 1850. Grand Ball at Devonshire House (detail). (R.903)

117. 1850. The County Hunt Ball in the New Hall, Reading (detail). (R.901)

1855

118. 1855. Walking costume and day dress. (R.874)

119. 1855. Day dresses. (R.873)

120. 1855. Walking costumes. (R.875)

121. 1855. Evening dresses. (R.1280)

122. 1855. Evening dresses. (R.871)

123, 124. 1855. State Ball at Windsor Castle (details). (K.2888)

125. 1855. Queen Victoria at the ball at the Hôtel de Ville, Paris (detail). (R.972)

1860

126. 1860. Day dresses. (R.1053)

127. 1860. Walking costumes. (R.1052)

128. *c.*1860. Full evening dresses. (R.1050)

129. *c.*1860. Evening dresses. (R.1049)

130. 1860. Evening dresses. (R. 1048)

131, 132. 1858. Corset (front and back).

133. 1859. Scene at a fête (cartoon, detail). (R.1281)

135. 1860. Scene at a dance (cartoon, detail). (R.1026)

134. 1860. Scene in Hyde Park (cartoon, detail). (R.1024)

1865

136. 1865. Walking dresses. (R.933)

137. 1865. Day dress and walking costume. (R.930)

138. 1865. Walking costumes. (R.932)

139. 1865. Evening dress and walking dress. (R.1056)

140. 1865. Evening dresses. (R.931)

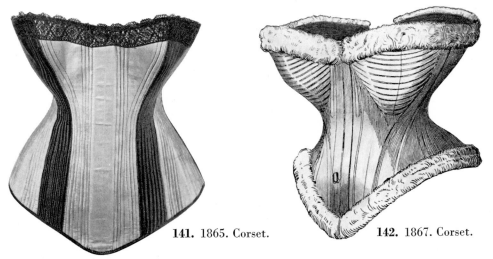

141. 1865. Corset.   **142.** 1867. Corset.

143. 1865. Women and a crinoline cage (cartoon, detail). (R.1031)

144. 1865. Croquet scene (cartoon). (R.1028)

145. 1865. Scene at a dance (cartoon). (R.1030)

1870

146. 1870. Walking costumes. (R.953)

147. 1870. Day dresses. (R.951)

148. 1870. Walking costumes. (R.952)

149. 1870. Full evening dresses. (R.948)

150. 1870. Full evening dresses. (R.949)

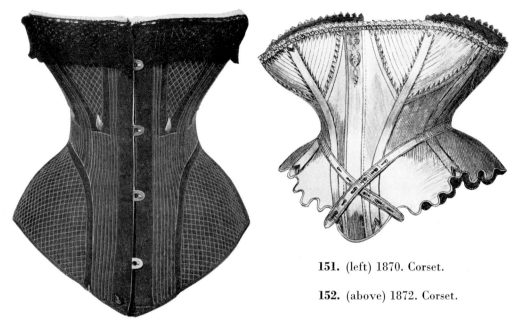

151. (left) 1870. Corset.

152. (above) 1872. Corset.

153. 1873. Scene before a dance (detail).

154. 1870. Scene at a dance (cartoon). (R.1283)

155. 1870. Scene at the seaside (cartoon, detail).
(R.1282)

1875

156. 1875. Day dresses. (R.989)

157. 1875. Day dresses. (R.895)

158. 1875. Walking dresses. (R.893)

159. 1875. Day dress and evening dress. (R.891)

160. 1875. Full evening dresses. (R.892)

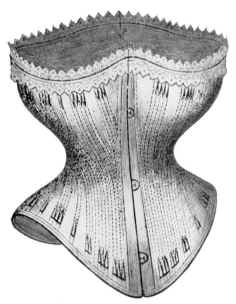

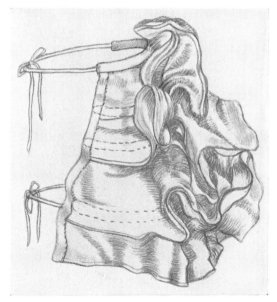

161. 1875. Corset. (R.889)

162. 1875. Bustle.

163. 1875. Scene at the seaside (cartoon, detail). (R.1032) **164.** 1875. Travelling scene
(cartoon, detail). (R.1033)

165. *c.*1875. *Ball on Shipboard* (detail).

166, 167. 1873. Scene at an American reception (details). (R.927)

1880

168. Promenade dresses. (R.974)

169. 1880. Travelling costume. (R.954)   **170.** 1880. Travelling costume. (R.975)

171. 1880. Walking costume. (R.955)   **172.** 1880. Ball dress. (R.973)

173. 1880. Evening dress and ball dress. (R.981)

174. 1880. Dinner dress and evening dress. (R.977)

175. 1880. Corset.　　　　　　　　　　**176.** 1878. Corset.

177. 1880. Scene at a milliner's (cartoon). (R.1284)

178. 1879. Scene at a ball (cartoon, detail). (R.1034)

179. 1880. Domestic scene (cartoon). (R.1035)

148

1885

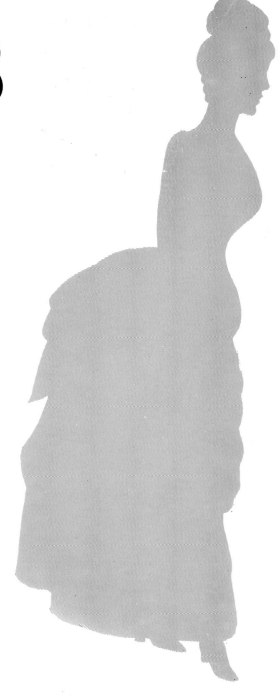

180. 1885. Day dress. (R.785)

181. 1885. Day dress. (R.784)

182. 1885. Outdoor costumes. (R.1046)

183. 1885. Dinner dresses. (R.1044)

184. 1885. Ball dresses. (R.1043)

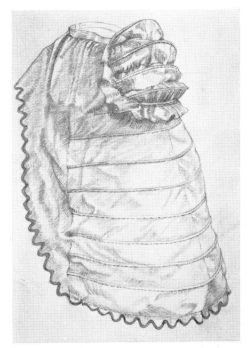

185. 1885. Corset. (R.1047) **186.** *c.*1885. Bustle.
187. 1885. Scene in Hyde Park (cartoon). (R.1036)

188. *c.*1885. A musical evening (detail). (R.990)

1890

189. 1890. Promenade dresses. (R.916)

190. 1890. Promenade dresses. (R.913)

191. 1890. Walking dress. (R.787)   **192.** 1890. Walking dress. (R.791)

193. 1890. Evening dresses. (R.912)

194. 1890. Day dresses and full evening dresses. (R.917)

195. 1890. Ball dresses. (R.915)

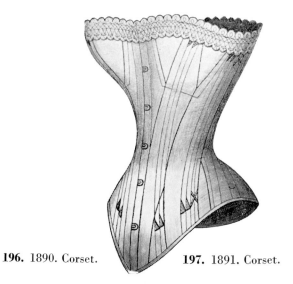

196. 1890. Corset.   **197.** 1891. Corset.

198. 1890. Scene at Hurlingham (detail). (R.982)

1895

199. 1895. Country dresses. (R.922)

200. 1895. Outdoor costume. (R.921)

201. 1895. Day costume and evening dresses. (R.920)

202. 1895. Outdoor costumes. (R.924)

203. 1895. Full evening dresses. (R.925)

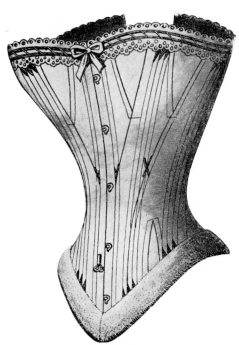

204. 1893. Corset.   **205.** 1895. Corset. (R.926)

206. 1895. Scene at Ascot. (R.983)

207. 1895. Scene at an evening party (cartoon). (R.1040)
208. 1895. Scene at a dance (cartoon). (R.1038)

1900

209. 1900. Day dress. (R.937)　　　　**210.** 1900. Outdoor costume. (R.938)

211. 1900. Tailor-made costume and outdoor costume. (R.1265)

212. 1900. Day dress. (R.942)

213. 1900. Evening dress. (R.1263)

214. 1900. Ball dress. (R.936)

215. 1900. Corset. (R.1269)   **216.** 1901. Corset.

217. 1900. The Prince and Princess of Wales at the Mansion House (detail). (R.1062)

219. 1900. Scene at a dance (cartoon, detail). (R.1060)

218. 1900. Scene in the country (cartoon, detail). (R. 1061)

SHORT BIBLIOGRAPHY

Boehn, M. von. *Modes and Manners of the Nineteenth Century.* Translated by M. Edwardes, 4 vols. 1909.

Webb, W. M. *The Heritage of Dress.* 1912.

Bott, A., and Clephane, I. *Our Mothers, 1870–1900.* 1932.

Libron, F., and Clouzot, H. *Le Corset dans l'Art et les Mœurs du XIIIe au XXe Siècle.* 1933.

Young, G. M. (ed.) *Early Victorian England, 1830–65.* 2 vols. 1934.

Cunnington, C. Willett. *Feminine Attitudes in the Nineteenth Century.* 1936.

Quennell, Peter. *Victorian Panorama.* 1937.

Flugel, J. C. *The Psychology of Clothes.* 2nd ed. 1940.

Laver, J. *Taste and Fashion.* 2nd ed. 1945.

Cunnington, C. Willett. *English Women's Clothing in the Nineteenth Century.* New Impression. 1948.

Cunnington, C. Willett and P. *Handbook of English Costume in the Nineteenth Century* (men and women). 1959.

Periodicals

The Gallery of Fashion (Heideloff). 1794–1803.

Journal des Dames et des Modes. 1797–1839.

The Ladies' Monthly Museum. 1798–1832.

The Lady's Magazine. 1800–39.

La Belle Assemblée. 1806–32, 1834–50.

Ackermann's Repository. 1809–29.

Petit Courrier des Dames. 1822–65.

La Mode. 1829–54.

Le Bon Ton. 1834–74.

Journal des Demoiselles. 1834–92.

Punch. 1841–1900.

Illustrated London News. 1844–1900.

Englishwoman's Domestic Magazine. 1854–79.

Le Monde Élegant. 1856–82.

The Ladies' Treasury. 1858–94.

La Mode Illustrée. 1860–19(?).

The Queen. 1863–1900.

La Mode Artistique. 1869–99.

The Sketch. 1893–1900.

SOURCES OF THE ILLUSTRATIONS
AND ACKNOWLEDGMENTS

(NOTE: the numbers refer to the Figures, not the pages.)

FASHION PLATES

Gallery of Fashion, 1, 2, 3, 4.

Fashions, 5, 6.

The Lady's Magazine, 14, 15, 16, 17, 18, 19.

La Belle Assemblée, 21, 35, 36, 40, 68, 69, 70, 71, 72.

Ackermann's Repository, 22, 23, 24, 25, 26, 27, 34, 37, 38, 39, 46, 47, 48, 49, 50, 51, 52, 53, 57, 58, 59, 60, 61, 62, 63, 64.

Petit Courrier des Dames, 80, 81, 82, 83, 84, 89, 90, 91, 92, 93, 98, 99, 100, 101, 102, 108, 109, 110, 111, 112, 118, 119, 120, 121, 122.

Le Génie de la Mode, 126

Le Monde Élegant, 127, 128, 129, 130.

The Young Englishwoman, 136, 137, 138, 140.

Englishwoman's Domestic Magazine, 139.

The Milliner and Dressmaker, 146, 147, 148, 149.

Le Bon Ton, 150.

La Mode Illustrée, 156, 157, 158, 159, 160, 168, 170, 172, 174.

The Queen, 173, 189, 190, 193, 194, 195, 199, 200, 201, 202, 203, 209, 210, 212, 213, 214.

Revue de la Mode, 182, 183, 184, 191.

Le Mode Artisique, 180, 181.

L'Art et la Mode, 192.

Fashion plates of unidentified source, 171, 211.

CORSETS AND BUSTLES

28, 29. from *Le Corset dans L'Art et les Mœurs du XIIIe au XXe Siècle*, by F. Libron and H. Clouzot. Paris, 1933. By kind permission of Libron et Cie., Paris.

30. detail from an engraving, 'Progress of the Toilet – the Stays', by J. Gillray (1810).

31. detail from an engraving, 'La Fureur des Corsets' (c.1809).

73. detail from a lithograph 'La Marchande de Corsets' (1830).

74. detail from a lithograph, 'Le Lacet' (1830).

85. detail from a fashion plate (*Le Petit Courrier des Dames*) (1837). By kind permission of the Radio Times-Hulton Picture Library.

94, 95. from Libron and Clouzot (op. cit.).

103, 104. from Libron and Clouzot (op. cit.).

113. detail from a lithograph, 'La Lionne' (1850).

114. from Libron and Clouzot (op. cit.).

131, 132. from photgraphs of a Symington corset. By kind permission of Messrs. R. and W. H. Symington & Co. Ltd. of Market Harborough.

141. from a photograph of a Symington corset.

142. from Libron and Clouzot (op. cit.).

151. from a photograph of a Symington corset.

152. from Libron and Clouzot (op. cit.).

161. from a contemporary advertisement.

162. from a drawing kindly made and supplied by Miss D. C. J. Glinos.

175. from a contemporary advertisement.

176. from Libron and Clouzot (op. cit.).

185. from a contemporary advertisement.

186. from a drawing kindly made and supplied by Miss D. C. J. Glinos.

196. from a photograph of a Symington corset.

204. from Libron and Clouzot (op. cit.).

205. from a contemporary advertisement.

215. from a contemporary advertisement.

216. from Libron and Clouzot (op. cit.).

SCENES, ETC.

7, 8, 9. details from a water-colour by T. Rowlandson of 'Boodle's Club fete to George III at Ranelagh'. By kind permission of Messrs. Frank T. Sabin.

10. detail from an engraving, 'Parisian Ladies in their Winter Dress for 1800'.

11. detail from an engraving, 'Promenade de Longchamps' (1802).

20. detail from an engraving accompanying a song, 'One half of the world don't know how t'other lives' (1805).

32. detail from an engraving, 'The Graces in a high Wind' (1810).

33. detail from an engraving, 'The Rivals', by T. Rowlandson (1812).

42. detail from an illustration, 'The Breakfast', in *Poetical Sketches of Scarborough* (1813).

43. detail from an illustration, 'The Library' in *Poetical Sketches of Scarborough* (1813).

44. from an engraving 'La Famille Anglaise à Paris' (1816).

45. from an engraving, 'Le Bon Genre' (1814).

54. detail from an illustration by I. R. and G. Cruickshank, 'Tom and Jerry at the Exhibition of pictures at the Royal Academy', in *Life in London*, by P. Egan (1821).

55. detail from an illustration by I. R. and G. Cruickshank, 'Tom and Jerry in the Saloon at Covent Garden', in *Life in London*, by P. Egan (1821).

56. from a painting, 'The Cooke Family', by D. H. Parry. By kind permission of the Leicester Galleries, London.

65, 66. details from an illustration, 'The Royal Wells, Cheltenham', by Robert Cruickshank, in *The English Spy*, by B. Blackmantle (1826).

67. details from an illustration, 'The Cyprians Ball at the Argyll Rooms', by Robert Cruickshank, in *The English Spy*, by B. Blackmantle (1826).

75. from a painting, 'At the Shoemaker's', by an anonymous artist. By kind permission of the Leicester Galleries, London.

76–79. from four caricatures.

87. detail from a lithograph, 'Opening of New Hungerford Market', by A. W. Billings. By kind permission of the Trustees of the British Museum.

88. from a painting of 'The Grosvenor Family', by C. R. Leslie. By kind permission of the Executors of the late Duke of Westminster.

96. detail from a lithograph, 'Hyde Park, near Grosvenor Gate', by T. S. Boys.

97. detail from a lithograph, 'Soirér Musicale', by A. Devéria (1840).

105. detail from a cartoon in *Punch* (1845). With grateful acknowledgments to the proprietors of *Punch*.

115. detail from a lithograph, 'Transept of the Great Exhibition Building from the Principal Refreshment Court', by L. Haghe.

116. detail from an illustration in *The Illustrated London News* (1850). With grateful acknowledgment to the proprietors of the *Illustrated London News*.

117. detail from an illustration in *The Illustrated London News* (1850).

123, 124. details from an illustration in *The Illustrated London News* (1855).

125. detail from an illustration in *L'Illustration* (1855). With grateful acknowledgment to the proprietors of *L'Illustration*.

133–135. details from three cartoons in *Punch* (1860).

143–145. details from three cartoons in *Punch* (1865).

153. detail from a painting 'Too Early', by J. J. Tissot. By kind permission of the Director of the Guildhall Art Gallery.

154, 155. from two cartoons (one a detail) in *Punch* (1870).

163, 164. details from two cartoons in *Punch* (1874).

165. detail from a painting, 'Ball on Shipboard', by J. J. Tissot. By kind permission of the Trustees of the Tate Gallery.

166, 168. details from an illustration in *The Illustrated London News* (1873).

177–179. details from three cartoons in *Punch* (1880; 1879; 1880).

187. from a cartoon in *Punch* (1885).

188. detail from a drawing, 'Scene in a Drawing Room', by Charles H. Shannon, R.A.

198, 206. details from two illustrations in *The Graphic* (1890; 1895).

207, 208. details from two cartoons in *Punch* (1895).

217. detail from an illustration in *The Illustrated London News* (1900).

218, 219. details from two cartoons in *Punch* (1900).

Dd. 138202   K80